SOCCER SKILLS AND DRILLS

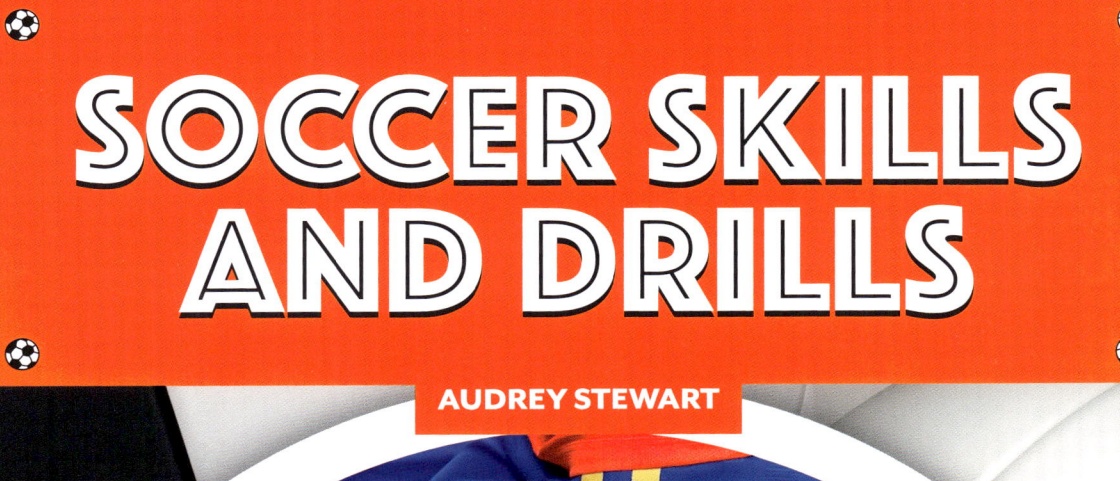

AUDREY STEWART

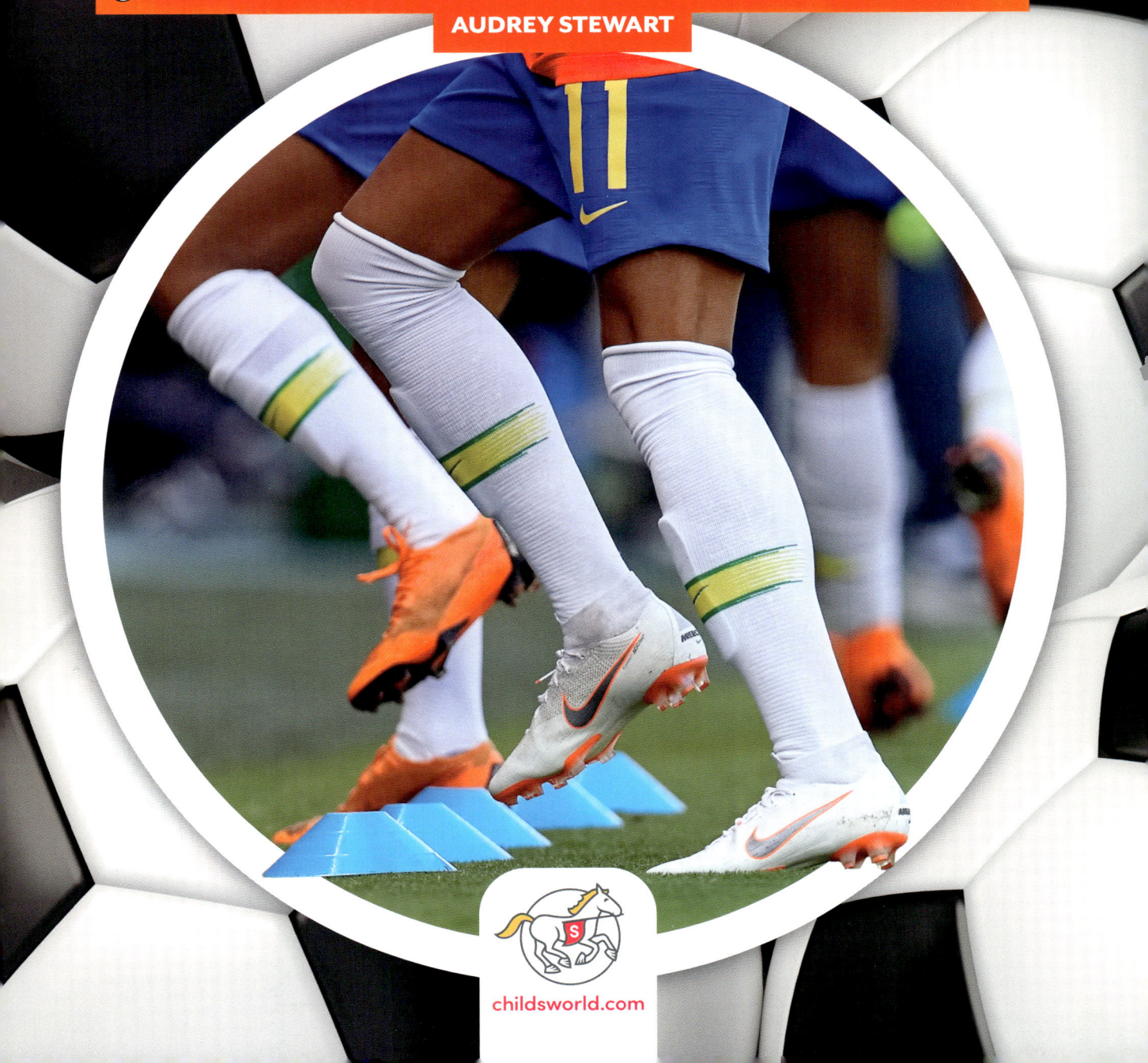

childsworld.com

The Child's World®
childsworld.com

Published by The Child's World®
800-599-READ · childsworld.com

Photography Credits
Cover: ©Icon Sportswire/Getty Images; ©AlexeyVS/Getty Images; page 4: ©Kleber Cordeiro/Shutterstock; page 5: ©AzmcnJaka/Getty Images; page 6: ©irin-k/Shutterstock; page 7: ©RTimages/Getty Images; page 7: ©Halfpoint/Getty Images; page 8: ©Pictures from History/Getty Images; page 9: ©Ivcandy/Getty Images; page 11: ©vm/Getty Images; page 13: ©Lumi Images/Dario Secen/Getty Images; page 14: ©Nigel French/PA Images/Getty Images; page 15: ©DEA/ICAS94/Getty Images; page 17: ©FG Trade/Getty Images; page 19: The Good Brigade/Getty Images; page 19: ©Tim Nwachukwu/Getty Images; page 22: ©Koonsiri Boonnak/Shutterstock; page 23: ©Koonsiri Boonnak/Shutterstock; page 25: ©FatCamera/Getty Images; page 27: ©Morsa Images/Getty Images; page 28: ©Bestie Van der Meer/Getty Images; page 29: ©AlexanderNakic/Getty Images

ISBN Information
ISBN 9781503894303 (Reinforced Library Binding)
ISBN 9781503895256 (Portable Document Format)
ISBN 9781503896079 (Online Multi-user eBook)
ISBN 9781503896895 (Electronic Publication)

LCCN
2024941408

Printed in the United States of America

ABOUT THE AUTHOR
Audrey Stewart is a writer, educator, and librarian who has a strong belief that stories have the power to open our minds and connect us all. She writes nonfiction, including a children's series about her years of rescuing stray animals. She lives in San Antonio, Texas, with her husband and their four rescued critters.

CONTENTS

INTRODUCTION

Every soccer player in the world, from seasoned players to rising stars, starts with the basics. Soccer players must learn basic skills and practice them all the time. Some skills are physical, and some involve how to work with others as a team. Physical skills include **dribbling** the ball, passing to teammates with both short and long passes, shooting to score from different angles, ball control, body awareness, and **tackling**. Being a great team player includes practicing mental and emotional skills. This means respecting coaches, showing up on time to practice and games, and being ready to play.

Players develop both sets of skills over time. Dribbling, passing, and shooting drills help them master the game. Playing on a team helps players learn how to work with others. Over time, players who focus on these basics can take their game to the next level.

More than 250 million people around the world play soccer regularly.

CHAPTER ONE

THE BASICS

Getting better at anything in life requires practice. Even **professional** soccer players practice daily. Before soccer practice can begin, players need some basic safety equipment. Believe it or not, this includes shoes. Wearing the right shoes is important! Soccer players need supportive, well-fitting shoes with cleats, or tiny plastic spikes, on the bottom. These help the players grip the field when they are running. Players also need shin guards, and some choose to wear a mouth guard. Shin guards are pieces of hard plastic that slide into a player's socks to protect their lower legs. Mouth guards protect their teeth. Since soccer is a contact sport, shin and mouth guards keep players safe from the ball and other players.

When players are ready to practice, they should make sure their water bottles are full. Staying **hydrated** during sports is important, especially on warm days. Safety also includes stretching before practicing. Stretching tells the body and the brain that it is time to exercise and move. This can protect players from injuries.

Having the right equipment is part of playing any game.
Comfort and safety are the first steps to learning the basic skills.

HISTORY OF SOCCER

Some historians believe that soccer is one of the oldest team sports ever played. Professional organized soccer dates back to the 1800s. But the idea of soccer might be traced back to the Aztecs over 2,000 years ago! It is possible that the ancient community used a rubber ball to kick back and forth. Other historians think soccer began in ancient China as a military training sport. It was known as cuju.

Once players are ready, it's time to practice. The most important item a player needs to play soccer is a ball. At a team practice, each player should have their own ball. Ball size varies based on the age of the players. Other basic equipment includes small cones and a net or goal. Cones are used for a variety of drills, and the goal is used for target practice. Players practice shooting the ball into the net or through the cones from different spots on the field.

The soccer field has lines so players know what is inbounds and out-of-bounds at the **sidelines**. Lines on the field also show the goal area, the **penalty box**, and the center circle where the game begins. The center circle is also used after each goal to restart the match.

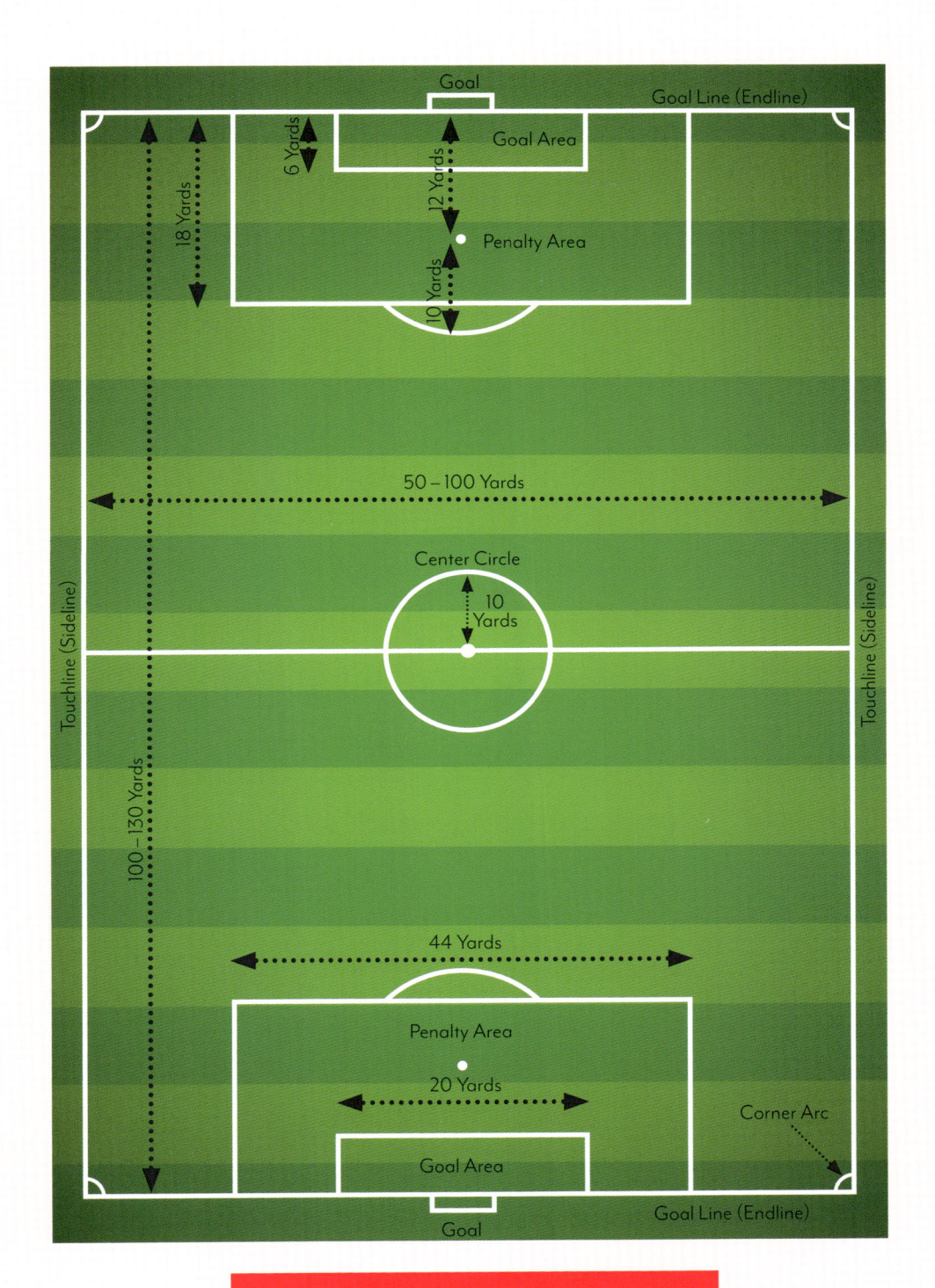

STANDARD SOCCER FIELD

CHAPTER TWO

PLAYING THE GAME

Knowing how soccer works is a skill. When players understand the rules, they can practice with game time in mind.

A soccer game begins with a coin toss. One team picks heads and the other picks tails. This determines who gets the ball first. There are up to 11 players on the field for each team, but youth teams can have as few as five, seven, or nine players.

The game starts when the ball is passed from one **forward** to another on the same team. Behind these players are **midfielders**. A third row includes **defenders**, and the goalkeeper is in the goal area. Games have two halves. A professional soccer match includes two 45-minute halves. Halves in youth games can be between 25 and 40 minutes depending on the age of the players. All teams have at least one coach. The coach is responsible for helping players with safety, equipment, and understanding the game. They help players get better through skills, drills, and teamwork. Games also have at least one **referee** to make sure everyone is following the rules.

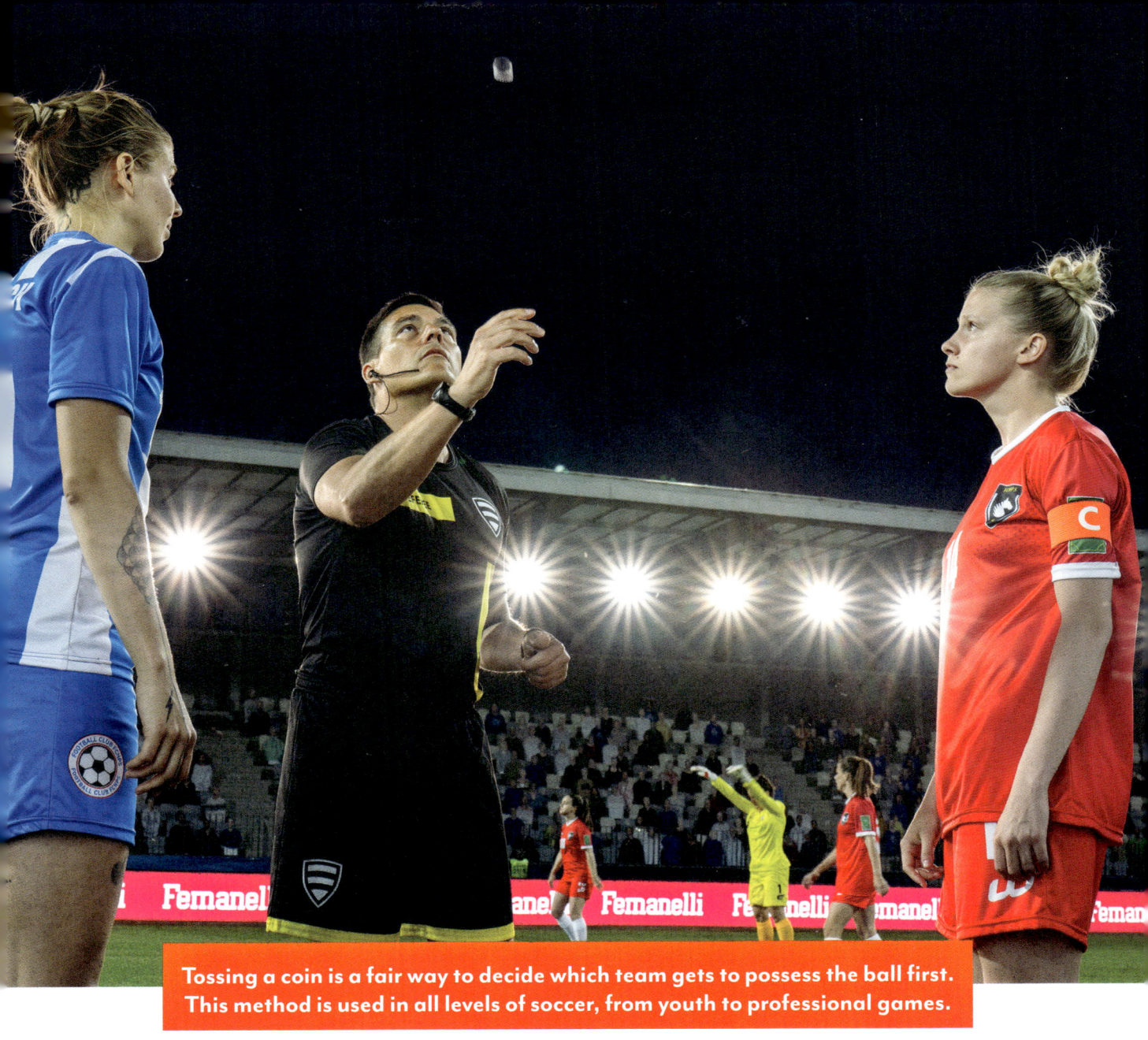

Tossing a coin is a fair way to decide which team gets to possess the ball first. This method is used in all levels of soccer, from youth to professional games.

Soccer's main and most basic rule is that field players cannot use their hands to move the ball down the field. They can use their heads, knees, hips, and chest. But if the ball touches any part of a player's arm, the referee will blow the whistle. This is called a handball and will result in a **free kick** for the other team.

Soccer is a contact sport. That means players might collide with each other or fall. But there are limits on what players can do. Tripping, pushing, or kicking a player are some examples of things that are against the rules. These are called fouls. When a player commits a foul, the other team gets a free kick. If a player commits a foul on purpose, they could get a yellow or red card. A yellow card is a warning. Players who are shown a yellow card can continue playing. If a player is shown a red card, they must leave the game.

When the defense commits a foul or handball inside the penalty box, the other team gets to shoot a **penalty kick**. This means the offensive player gets to take a shot a short distance from the goal. Only the goalkeeper can try to defend the shot.

During a free kick, players from the other team get a chance to defend their goal. During a penalty kick, only the goalie stands between the ball and the goal.

Corner kicks give teams a chance to score by placing the ball right in front of the other team's goal.

Soccer is played inside the field lines. When the ball goes out on the sideline, the referee determines which team made the ball go out of bounds. The other team throws the ball in to continue playing. The player must keep both feet on the ground when taking a throw-in.

If the ball goes out over the goal line, either a goal kick or corner kick is called, depending on which team it touched last. A goal kick occurs when a player kicks the ball across the other team's goal line. A corner kick occurs when a player kicks the ball across their own goal line.

MODERN SOCCER?

Modern soccer as it is played today began in England in the late 1800s. The first rules were created in 1848. The first professional league was organized in 1863. It was called the Football Association (FA). In most parts of the world, soccer is known as football. By the early 1900s, factory workers used soccer as a way to be social. The game has seen some rule changes over the years but has only grown more popular with time. Today, there are professional teams all over the world.

CHAPTER THREE

SPORTSMANSHIP

One of the most important skills an athlete can practice is sportsmanship. Sportsmanship means having respect for the game, the rules, coaches, other players, and referees. It even means being respectful to those who are watching the game. Showing kindness to another team is one example of good sportsmanship. Helping a player up after a fall, saying only positive or encouraging words, and shaking hands after the game are examples of sportsmanship. Another example is staying calm when the referee makes a call the team might not agree with.

Developing sportsmanship can be hard because it isn't as easy to practice as dribbling the ball. Taking a deep breath during a tough game can help players reset how they might be feeling. It can also be helpful to talk to teammates about frustrating moments during games or practices. Making good choices in these moments can help players get better at this important skill. And sportsmanship is helpful both on and off the field. Being a good sport can help players be better friends, siblings, and students.

Sportsmanship includes supporting fellow teammates. It also involves showing respect and kindness to opponents.

CHAPTER FOUR

FITNESS, NUTRITION, AND WELLNESS

Practicing skills and running through drills are important. But one of the most important parts of a player's performance happens before practice even starts. Eating nourishing foods and staying hydrated is a major part of being an athlete. Balanced meals and healthy snacks give athletes the fuel they need at practice. Staying hydrated with water and other healthy drink options is important for brain function and keeping muscles loose.

Sleep is another key element of athletic training. Sleep impacts the brain and mood. While an athlete sleeps, their brain unloads the things they learned that day. Their mood and emotions reset. Sleep and nutrition can also impact a player's mental wellness. Feeling good starts with nutrition, hydration, and sleep. Sometimes players can push themselves too hard, leading to exhaustion and even burnout. By paying attention to their body's needs, players can make smart decisions on the field.

MENTAL HEALTH MATTERS

Olympic gymnast Simone Biles is an example of an athlete who has been open about the importance of mental wellness. During the 2020 Tokyo Olympics, Biles opted out of competing in multiple events. She hadn't been listening to her body or her mental health and knew she was not herself. She desperately needed a break. Biles took a break on the world's biggest sports stage to pay attention to what her body needed. She knew it was more important to stay safe and not get injured.

Eating regular meals, drinking plenty of water, and getting a good night's sleep are as important to an athlete's training plan as stretching.

CHAPTER FIVE

OFFENSIVE SKILLS AND DRILLS

Dribbling, passing, and shooting are three important offensive skills. These three drills can help players get better at offense. Dribbling the ball is a key skill for players to master.

Try this: Place the ball on the ground. Tap the ball with the tip of one shoe. Then, place that foot down and repeat with the other foot. Increase speed as this gets easier. This drill helps players with ball control.

Try this: Lightly tap the ball while jogging. Keep the ball close—it is easier to control that way. When this feels easy, line up several cones. Dribble around each one without losing control of the ball.

Passing the ball short and long distances is an important game-time skill. Receiving the ball from a teammate involves using the side of your foot to slow down the pass or the bottom of your foot to trap the ball. This brings the ball to a complete stop.

Controlling the ball is a basic skill that all players must master.

Try this: Pass the ball back and forth to a teammate. Start out close together. Stop the ball with the inside of the foot. Then, gently pass it back. Try making 25 passes without missing. Try moving farther apart without losing control of the passes.

Next, it's time to practice shooting the ball. Shooting, or kicking the soccer ball at the goal, is an important drill.

Try this: Set up cones or use a net to aim for a goal. Practice using each foot to kick the ball between the cones or into the net. The cones can also be used to set a point to aim for. Kicking a goal from different angles will help players feel what a game situation might be like.

Players in any position on the field can score, so shooting drills are helpful for everyone on the team.

During a game, players need to be aware of their teammates at all times. This means that all players need to have position awareness. Forwards, midfielders, and defenders move up and down the field together in basically the same formation. All players go after the ball in their area to gain possession.

Try this: With your teammates or friends, choose a position to try. Pass the ball back and forth toward the goal, but stay in your position. Next, move toward the other goal and shift back down the field.

Moving from offense to defense happens quickly. When it comes to the next move, smart players are good at making decisions in the moment. Any player can end up in a position to pass, shoot, or dribble to move the ball away from the other team and toward their goal.

Practicing in small groups helps players prepare for game situations.

CHAPTER SIX

DEFENSIVE SKILLS AND DRILLS

Marking (guarding) a player, clearing the ball, knowing boundaries without fouling, and tackling are four skills that players can work on to get better at defense. When players are on defense, they need to mark the **opponent**. Defenders will mark the opposite team's forwards or midfielders who come into their space.

Try this: Position yourself next to another player as they move the ball. Stay next to them the entire time and try to get the ball back. Make sure they don't score!

Players on defense might clear the ball when the opposing team and the ball are close to scoring. Clearing the ball means kicking away from the other team's offense.

Soccer is often a game of keep-away, and the team that wins the ball gets a chance to score. Playing keep-away is a fun way to practice soccer defense.

Try this: Make sure there is space between you and the other players. Stand at one end of the field and kick the ball as hard as you can. Lean over the ball and get your toe slightly under it. This will help the ball go high and far.

While playing defense, players need to be careful not to foul their opponent. This requires strength and discipline. Charging an opponent, holding their jersey, or tackling them from behind are some examples of fouls.

To avoid a foul, focus on the ball. Tackling the ball with a sweeping motion is a safe play. Players might also block tackle, or move in front of a player to stop the ball before it is kicked.

DEFENDING THE GOAL

The goalkeeper has to defend the net. This area is 8 yards long and 8 feet (2.43 meters) high! Goalkeepers wear padded gloves to protect their hands. These players must have great **spatial awareness** to cover the wide area of the net. The goalkeeper can use their hands inside the penalty box. They cannot use their hands when the ball is thrown in or kicked by their teammates. Goalkeepers have to take control of the incoming ball with their feet. Finally, they cannot hold the ball for more than six seconds when passing it to a teammate.

Try this: With another player, try to get the ball by sweeping your foot toward the ball. If that doesn't work, keep moving around your opponent until you get the ball. Keep your opponent from passing!

Players get better at defense by practicing with their teammates in a safe environment. Practice helps young players learn the limits of the game without fouling. This takes self-discipline, body awareness, and concentration on the ball.

Developing all of these important skills takes time and practice on the field. One way to get better is to join a team. Being on a team gives players the experience of being a teammate. It also gives them time to practice with players at different levels. Most middle and high schools have soccer teams. Most cities and towns also have teams through community programs such as the YMCA.

In soccer, juggling means to keep the ball from touching the ground using any part of the body except the hands and arms. Juggling is a great way to practice ball control, and you don't need a teammate—you can juggle anytime and anywhere!

But athletes can work on skills even if they aren't on a team or practicing with teammates. Kicking the ball against a wall is a great way to practice solo. Some players enjoy juggling the ball to get used to using more of their bodies. Players can practice these skills anywhere!

GLOSSARY

defender (dee-FEN-dur) a player who is guarding their goal

dribbling (DRIB-ling) moving the ball with your foot

forward (FOR-wurd) a player who plays near the other team's goal and tries to score

free kick (FREE KIK) a kick in any direction that is awarded when the other team commits a foul

hydrated (HY-dray-ted) having drunk enough water or other liquid, especially as it relates to physical activity

midfielder (MID-feeld-ur) a player who plays between the forwards and defenders and can both defend the goal and score

opponent (uh-POH-nunt) a player from the other team

penalty box (PEN-ul-tee BOKS) the marked area around the goalkeeper

penalty kick (PEN-ul-tee KIK) a free kick taken from the penalty spot inside the penalty box, awarded when the defending team commits a foul inside the penalty box of their own team; only the goalie is allowed to defend a penalty kick

professional (pro-FESH-uh-nul) an athlete who is paid to play a sport

referee (ref-ur-EE) the person in charge of making sure the players follow the rules

sidelines (SIDE-lynz) the long lines on either side of the field that run from goal line to goal line

spatial awareness (SPAY-shul uh-WAYR-nuss) understanding where your body is and how it is affected by other people or objects

tackling (TAK-ling) taking away the ball from your opponent's feet

FAST FACTS

⚽ The soccer field is called the pitch in other parts of the world.

⚽ The first professional soccer team in history was Sheffield Football Club in England.

⚽ The largest soccer stadium in the world is in North Korea. It is called Rungrado 1st of May Stadium.

⚽ Soccer is the most popular game in the world. The Men's World Cup holds the record for most-viewed sporting event, with the Women's World Cup not far behind.

ONE STRIDE FURTHER

⚽ Test your knowledge: Draw a picture showing one of the skills mentioned in the book. Show and teach someone this skill based on your drawing.

⚽ Ask your friends and family who their favorite soccer team is. Make a chart and see how many people like the same team.

⚽ Describe a time when you saw an athlete practicing good sportsmanship. Why is good sportsmanship important?

⚽ With 11 people on a team, there are a lot of players on the field! In a few sentences, explain why communication between teammates is so important.

FIND OUT MORE

IN THE LIBRARY

Buckley, James Jr. *It's a Numbers Game! Soccer: The Math Behind the Perfect Goal, the Game-Winning Save, and So Much More!* Washington, DC: National Geographic Kids, 2020.

Chaffee, Kim. *Courage in Her Cleats: The Story of Soccer Star Abby Wambach.* Salem, MA: Page Street Kids, 2023.

Latham, Andrew. *Soccer Smarts for Teens: 50 Skills and Strategies to Master the Game.* Emeryville, CA: Rockridge Press, 2021.

ON THE WEB

Visit our website for links about soccer skills and drills:
childsworld.com/links

Note to Parents, Caregivers, Teachers, and Librarians: We routinely verify our web links to make sure they are safe and active sites. So encourage your readers to check them out!

INDEX